THE POP/ROCK

PIANO · VOCAL · GUITAR

the '70s

ISBN 0-634-03575-4

HAL•LEONARD®
CORPORATION

7777 W. BLUEMOUND RD. P.O. BOX 13819 MILWAUKEE, WI 53213

Visit Hal Leonard Online at
www.halleonard.com

THE POP/ROCK ERA: THE '70s

CONTENTS

ABC

Words and Music by ALPHONSO MIZELL, FREDERICK PERREN,
DEKE RICHARDS and BERRY GORDY

AMIE

By CRAIG FULLER

Moderately, in two

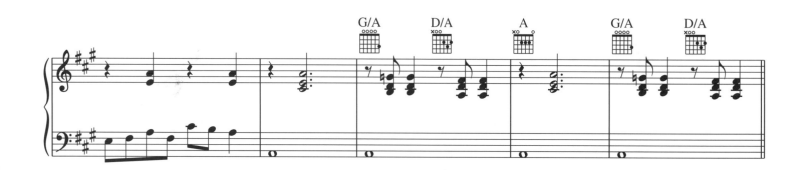

BABY, I LOVE YOUR WAY

Words and Music by
PETER FRAMPTON

BABY, I'M-A WANT YOU

Words and Music by
DAVID GATES

Used to be my life was just __ e - mo - tions pass - ing __ by, ___

feel-ing all the while and nev - er real - ly know-ing __ why. __

Late-ly, I'm a-pray-in' that you'll al - ways be __ a-stay-in' ___ be - side __

BEST OF MY LOVE

Words and Music by JOHN DAVID SOUTHER,
DON HENLEY and GLENN FREY

Moderately slow

Ev-er-y night ___ I'm ly-in' in bed, ___ hold-in' you close ___ in my
Beau-ti-ful faces and loud emp-ty places, look at the way that we

dreams; ___ think-in' a bout ___ all the things that we ___ said ___ and
live; ___ wast-in' our time ___ on cheap talk and wine

27

BOHEMIAN RHAPSODY

Words and Music by
FREDDIE MERCURY

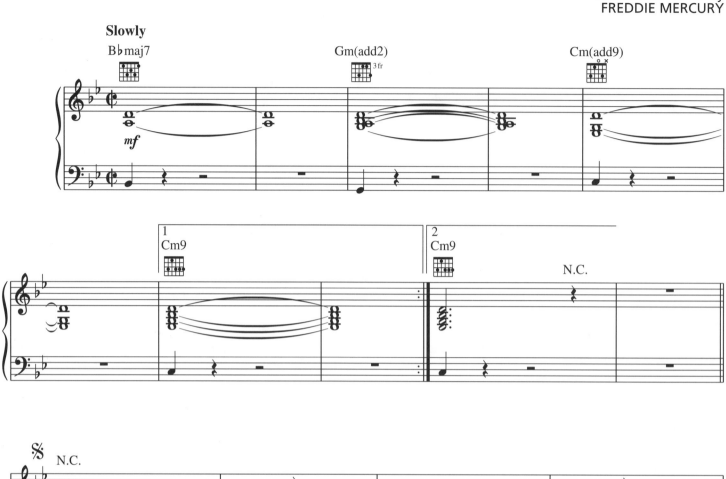

Ma - ma _____ just killed a man, _____ put a
Too late, _____ my time has come. _____ Sends

gun a - gainst his head, _____ pulled my trig - ger. Now, _ he's dead. _____
shiv - ers down _ my spine. _____ Bod - y's ach - ing all _____ the time. _____

DRIFT AWAY

Words and Music by
MENTOR WILLIAMS

DON'T CRY OUT LOUD

Words and Music by CAROLE BAYER SAGER
and PETER ALLEN

Don't cry __ out loud, _____ just keep it in - side, learn how to
Fly high __ and proud, _____ and if you should fall re - mem - ber you

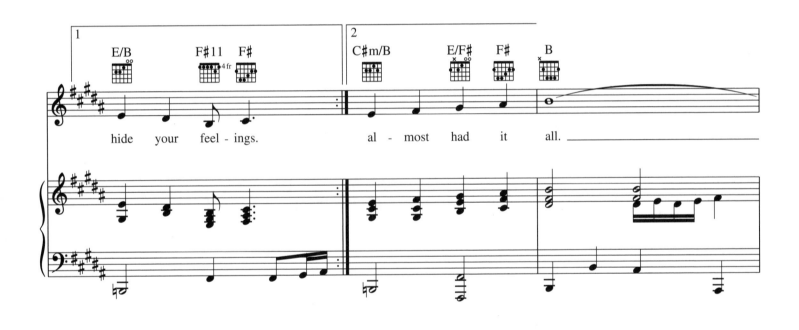

1
hide your feel - ings.

2
al - most had it all. _____

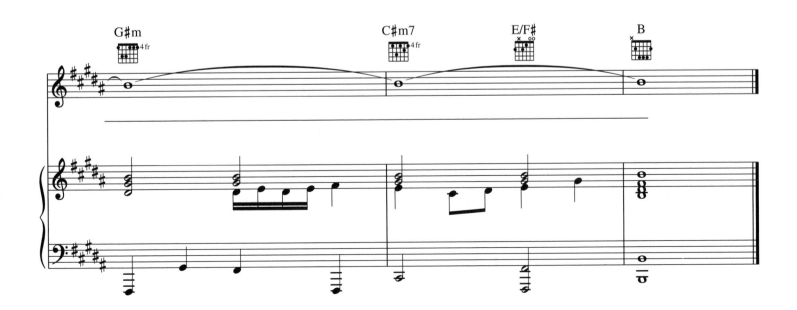

DUST IN THE WIND

Words and Music by
KERRY LIVGREN

ev - 'ry - thing _ is dust in the wind.
wind.)

Repeat and Fade

Optional Ending

poco rit.

FIRE AND RAIN

Words and Music by
JAMES TAYLOR

GOODBYE TO LOVE

Words and Music by RICHARD CARPENTER
and JOHN BETTIS

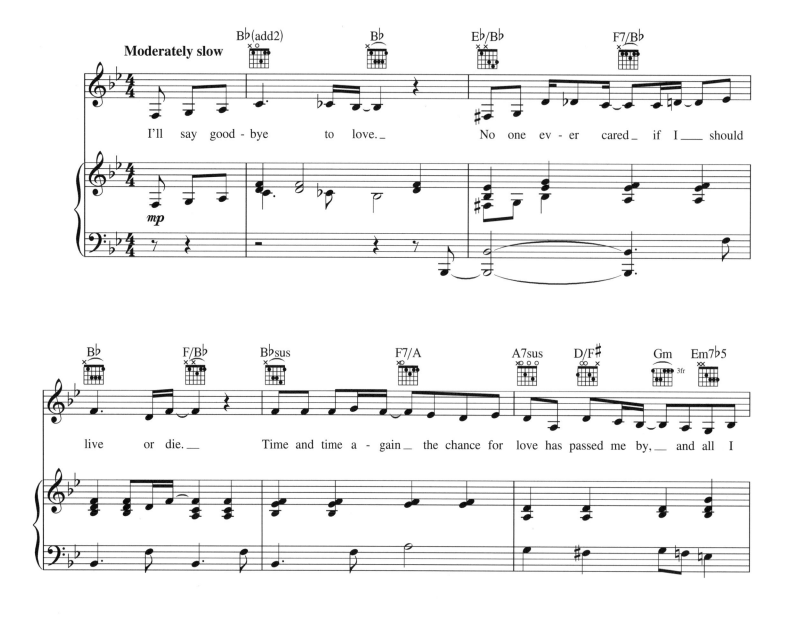

Repeat ad lib. and Fade

HOW DEEP IS YOUR LOVE

from the Motion Picture SATURDAY NIGHT FEVER

Words and Music by BARRY GIBB,
MAURICE GIBB and ROBIN GIBB

I HONESTLY LOVE YOU

Words and Music by PETER ALLEN
and JEFF BARRY

Lyrics (line 1):
May - be I hang a - round __ here a lit - tle more than I should; we both know I got some - where else __ to go. But

Lyrics (line 2):
You don't _ have to an - swer; I see it in your eyes. May - be it was bet - ter left __ un - said. But

HOW MUCH I FEEL

Words and Music by
DAVID PACK

*An optional ending is provided

I LOVE THE NIGHT LIFE

Words and Music by ALICIA BRIDGES
and SUSAN HUTCHESON

I'LL BE THERE

Words and Music by BERRY GORDY, HAL DAVIS,
WILLIE HUTCH and BOB WEST

JOY TO THE WORLD

Words and Music by
HOYT AXTON

I'LL NEVER LOVE THIS WAY AGAIN

Words and Music by RICHARD KERR
and WILL JENNINGS

IMAGINE

Words and Music by
JOHN LENNON

JIVE TALKIN'
from SATURDAY NIGHT FEVER

Words and Music by BARRY GIBB,
MAURICE GIBB and ROBIN GIBB

Moderately, with a strong beat

Tacet

It's just your jive talk - in', you're tell - in' me lies, __ yeah; jive talk - in', you wear a dis - guise. __

Jive talk - in', so mis - un - der - stood, __ yeah; jive talk - in', you're

JUST MY IMAGINATION
(Running Away with Me)

Words and Music by NORMAN J. WHITFIELD
and BARRETT STRONG

100

KILLING ME SOFTLY WITH HIS SONG

Words by NORMAN GIMBEL
Music by CHARLES FOX

104

THE LOGICAL SONG

Words and Music by RICK DAVIES
and ROGER HODGSON

Moderate Rock

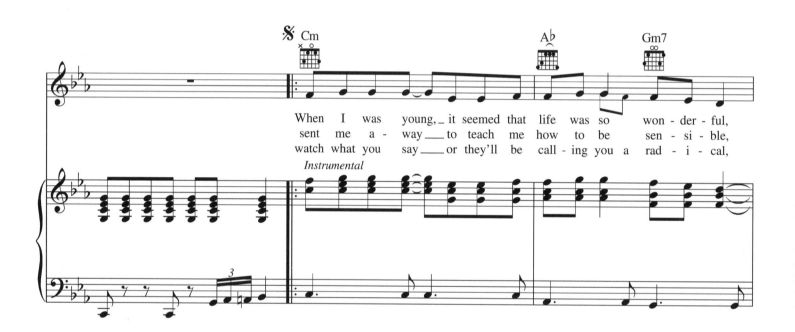

When I was young,_ it seemed that life was so won-der-ful,
sent me a-way_ to teach me how to be sen-si-ble,
watch what you say_ or they'll be call-ing you a rad-i-cal,

Instrumental

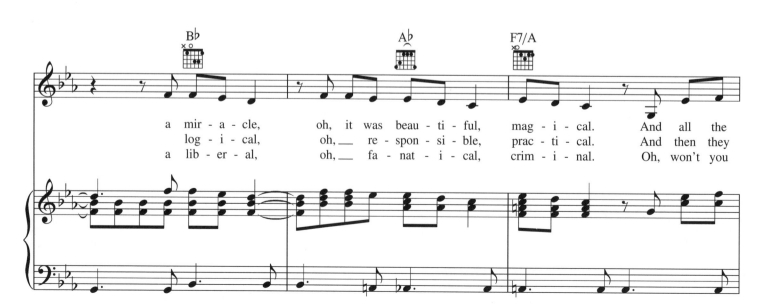

a mir-a-cle, oh, it was beau-ti-ful, mag-i-cal. And all the
log-i-cal, oh,_ re-spon-si-ble, prac-ti-cal. And then they
a lib-er-al, oh,_ fa-nat-i-cal, crim-i-nal. Oh, won't you

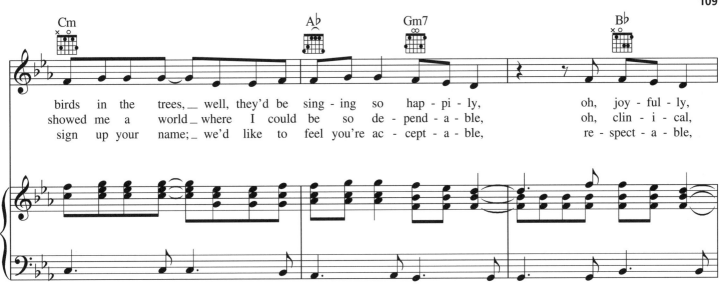

birds in the trees, __ well, they'd be sing-ing so hap-pi-ly,   oh, joy-ful-ly,
showed me a world __ where I could be so de-pend-a-ble,   oh, clin-i-cal,
sign up your name; __ we'd like to feel you're ac-cept-a-ble,   re-spect-a-ble,

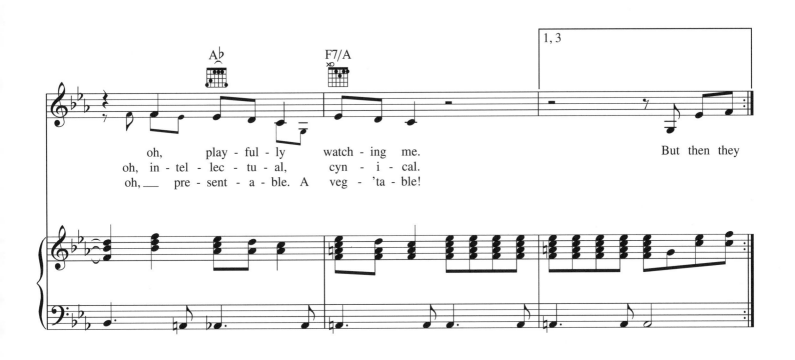

oh, play-ful-ly watch-ing me.   But then they
oh, in-tel-lec-tu-al, cyn-i-cal.
oh, __ pre-sent-a-ble. A veg-'ta-ble!

There are times __ }
Instrumental ends But at night, __ }   when all ___ the world's __ a-sleep, __

110

LOOKS LIKE WE MADE IT

Words and Music by RICHARD KERR
and WILL JENNINGS

1. There you are,— look-in' just the same as you did last time I
2. Love's so strange,— play-ing hide and seek with hearts and al-ways

touched you. And here I am,— close to get-tin' tan-gled up— in-side the
hurt-ing. And we're the fools,— stand-ing close e-nough to touch those burn-ing

thought of you. Do you love him as much as I— love her? And will that love be
mem-o-ries. And if I hold you for the sake of all— those times love made us lose our

LOVE THE ONE YOU'RE WITH

Words and Music by
STEPHEN STILLS

117

OPERATOR
(That's Not the Way It Feels)

Words and Music by
JIM CROCE

OUR HOUSE

Words and Music by
GRAHAM NASH

OYE COMO VA

Words and Music by
TITO PUENTE

PIANO MAN

Words and Music by
BILLY JOEL

RAINY DAYS AND MONDAYS

Lyrics by PAUL WILLIAMS
Music by ROGER NICHOLS

SEPTEMBER

Words and Music by MAURICE WHITE,
AL McKAY and ALLEE WILLIS

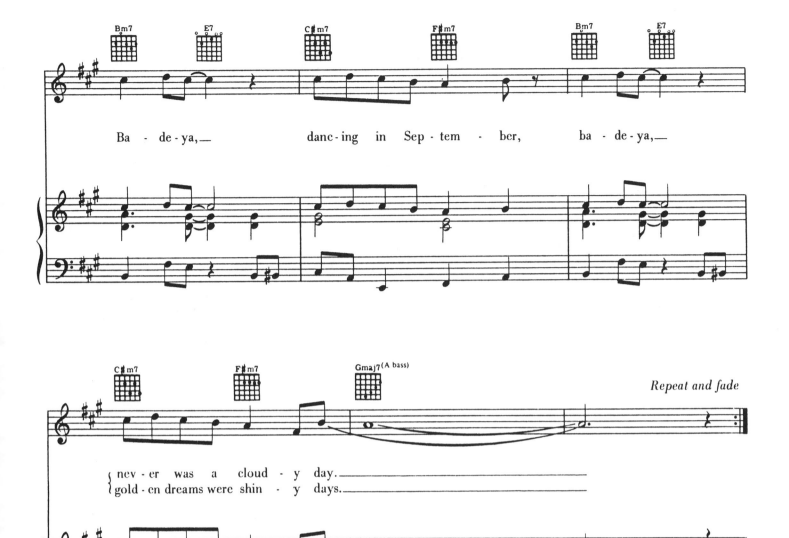

Ba - de - ya,— danc - ing in Sep - tem - ber, ba - de - ya,—

Repeat and fade

{ nev - er was a cloud - y day._____
{ gold - en dreams were shin - y days._____

3rd Verse

My thoughts are with you,
    holding hands with your heart,
    to see you, only blue talk and love.
Remember how we knew love was here to stay?

4th Verse

Now December found the love that we shared,
September, only blue talk and love.
Remember the true love we share today.

SIGNED, SEALED, DELIVERED I'M YOURS

Words and Music by STEVIE WONDER, SYREETA WRIGHT,
LEE GARRETT and LULA MAE HARDAWAY

CODA

8va

I could be a bro-ken man, but here I am with your fu-ture, got your fu-

-ture, babe; signed, sealed, de-liv-ered I'm yours.

Here I am ba-by, signed, sealed, de-liv-ered I'm yours.

Repeat and Fade **Optional Ending**

Here I am ba-by, signed, sealed, de-liv-ered I'm yours!

SIGNS

Words and Music by
LES EMMERSON

Sign, sign.

Repeat and Fade

Optional Ending

SO INTO YOU

Words and Music by BUDDY BUIE,
DEAN DAUGHTRY and ROBERT NIX

SOMEWHERE IN THE NIGHT

Words and Music by WILL JENNINGS
and RICHARD KERR

STAYIN' ALIVE
from the Motion Picture SATURDAY NIGHT FEVER

Words and Music by BARRY GIBB,
MAURICE GIBB and ROBIN GIBB

WE'VE ONLY JUST BEGUN

Words and Music by ROGER NICHOLS
and PAUL WILLIAMS

We've on-ly just be-gun _____ to live. _____

White lace and prom - i - ses, a kiss for luck _ and we're

on our way. _____

(1.) Be - fore the ris - ing
(2.,D.S.) And when the eve - ning

THREE TIMES A LADY

Words and Music by
LIONEL RICHIE

TIE A YELLOW RIBBON ROUND THE OLE OAK TREE

Words and Music by L. RUSSELL BROWN
and IRWIN LEVINE

TIME IN A BOTTLE

Words and Music by
JIM CROCE

192

WHEN WILL I BE LOVED

Words and Music by
PHIL EVERLY

YOU ARE SO BEAUTIFUL

Words and Music by BILLY PRESTON
and BRUCE FISHER

YOU AND ME AGAINST THE WORLD

Words and Music by PAUL WILLIAMS
and KEN ASCHER

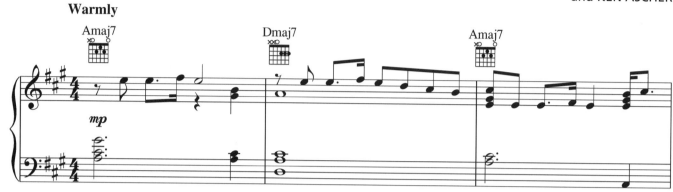

YOU MAKE ME FEEL LIKE DANCING

Words and Music by VINI PONCIA
and LEO SAYER